SECRETS OF
The Heartlands

DON BOSCO
Illustrated by Sharon Lei

Marshall Cavendish
Editions

Editor: Melvin Neo
Designer: Adithi Khandadai Shankar

© 2016 Don Bosco (Super Cool Books) and
Marshall Cavendish International (Asia) Pte Ltd

This book is published by Marshall Cavendish Editions in association with Super Cool Books
Marshall Cavendish Editions is an imprint of Marshall Cavendish International
1 New Industrial Road, Singapore 536196

Other Marshall Cavendish Offices:
Marshall Cavendish Corporation. 99 White Plains Road, Tarrytown NY 10591-9001, USA • Marshall
Cavendish International (Thailand) Co Ltd. 253 Asoke, 12th Flr, Sukhumvit 21 Road, Klongtoey Nua,
Wattana, Bangkok 10110, Thailand • Marshall Cavendish (Malaysia) Sdn Bhd, Times Subang, Lot 46,
Subang Hi-Tech Industrial Park, Batu Tiga, 40000 Shah Alam, Selangor Darul Ehsan, Malaysia

Marshall Cavendish is a trademark of Times Publishing Limited

National Library Board, Singapore Cataloguing-in-Publication Data
Names: Bosco, Don, 1971-. | Lei, Sharon, illustrator.
Title: Secrets of the heartlands / Don Bosco ; illustrated by Sharon Lei.
Other titles: Lion City adventures.
Description: Singapore : Marshall Cavendish Editions, [2016] | "This book is published by Marshall
Cavendish Editions in association with Super Cool Books."
Identifiers: OCN 926656654 | ISBN 978-981-4721-16-5 (paperback)
Subjects: LCSH: Singapore—Discovery and exploration—Juvenile literature.
Classification: LCC DS609.7 | DDC 915.95704—dc23

Printed in Singapore by Colourscan Print Co Pte Ltd

Contents

Map of Singapore   4
Introduction: Secrets of the Heartlands   5

Let's Learn About
The History of Toa Payoh   9
The History of Yishun   19
The History of Queenstown   29
The History of Tiong Bahru   39
The History of Kampong Bahru   49
The History of Jalan Kayu   59
The History of Marine Parade   69
The History of Punggol   79

The Secret Notebook: Conclusion   89
About the Author and Illustrator   94

MAP OF SINGAPORE

KEY
1. Jalan Kayu
2. Kampong Bahru
3. Marine Parade
4. Punggol
5. Queenstown
6. Toa Payoh
7. Tiong Bahru
8. Yishun

INTRODUCTION

The Lion City Adventuring Club (LCAC) was started in the year 1894. Its members focussed on three simple goals: to have fun exploring Singapore, make new friends and share interesting stories.

As the club grew, the members explored and made maps of the many interesting kampongs (Malay for "village") scattered all over the island, moving further and further out of the main city area.

Everywhere they went, they would encourage the children to start their own exploration groups and share their adventuring stories with the LCAC through letters and sketches.

In 1930, Chief Adventurer Gopal S., then a student and librarian at St. Joseph's Institution, invited three LCAC members to start the Special Council for the Greater Exploration of Kampongs (SCGFK). They organised weekly trips to visit even the most distant kampongs.

One of the members often borrowed her father's camera for the excursions. This was the beginning of the LCAC's photograph archive. It contains many unique and inspiring shots taken over the years.

In 1967, the SCGEK launched its own newsletter, the Lion City Journal of Open Exploration. Each issue contained exploration guides for different neighbourhoods, photographs of interesting landmarks, suggestions for activities, as well as adventuring reports submitted by the members.

As Singapore continued to develop, many of the kampong areas were cleared to make space for high rise apartments. In 1982, after many meetings, Chief Adventurer Janice De Cruz finally convinced the SCGEK leaders to change their focus. During the LCAC's Christmas party that year, they announced that they would henceforth be known as the Heartlands Exploration Group. Their new objective: to create a network of young and brave explorers all across the heartlands, and keep the kampong spirit alive.

In 2015, a retired businessman donated a very generous sum of money to support the LCAC's heartlands research activities. Thanks to him, the Heartlands Exploration Group was able to compile the best bits from its Lion City Journal of Open Exploration and publish this book for the enjoyment of young adventurers everywhere.

Why did the retired businessman do this?
It's an amazing story indeed.
And it starts in the next chapter.

CHAPTER 1

The History of
TOA PAYOH

1849 This area was called "Toah Pyoh" on a government map. (Read on to find out what this phrase meant.) It was mostly muddy ground. Not a safe place for children to play. Eventually some plantations were started here.

Early 1900s Toa Payoh's kampong (or village) era. There were many Chinese villages as well as some Malay kampongs. People were friendly and helpful.

1962 Bulldozers arrive to clear the kampongs. Singapore's first housing estate is built here, with its own market, shops and fun facilities.

1973 The SEAP Games was held over eight daysin Singapore. Part of Toa Payoh Central was transformed into the SEAP Games Village. (SEAP stands for Southeast Asian Peninsula. In 1977, it was renamed the SEA Games, or Southeast Asian Games.) Four blocks in Toa Payoh were used as dormitories for the athletes. Another building that was used for the Games Village eventually became the Toa Payoh Branch Library.

1972 Her Majesty Queen Elizabeth II of the United Kingdom visited a family living in Block 53. The children living nearby gathered to shout, "Long Live the Queen!"

TOA PAYOH
Land of the Dragon Playground

A long time ago, Toa Payoh was a great swampland. There were paths and crossings here and there, but it was mostly hard to move around.

In 1853, a British engineer and his team built the first big road through this area. His name was John Turnbull Thomson, and the road was named after him: Thomson Road.

This area became more popular after this. Some plantations were started, mostly to grow spices like pepper and nutmeg.

By around 1900, Chinese settlers started to move in. They lived in huts and grew their own food. Some families became known for making tofu (soy bean curd).

All the families in a kampong had to share a water pipe. There were always long queues around the pipe. Back home, the precious water was used very carefully, for cooking, cleaning and washing. Because of this, most people didn't get to bathe very often

During World War Two, the Japanese soldiers set up farms around Toa Payoh. They made local workers grow vegetables and tapioca as well as rear fish and pigs for them.

After the war, the kampongs were plagued by gangsters. They would fight in the streets very often. Even the police tried to keep away from them.

In the 1960s, the government started to move the kampong dwellers out. They turned the once-swampy area into a modern town, with impressive apartment blocks and a bustling town centre.

In 1970, the Great Royal Circus of India came to Toa Payoh. It set up its tent in a big field along Lorong 5. The children gathered to see the elephants, chimpanzees, bears, donkeys, lions and tigers. There were even some ligers, which are offspring of a male lion and a female tiger.

In 1979, the delightful Dragon Playground was built at Lorong 6. The early public playgrounds around Singapore were all inspired by animals, and this Dragon Playground was definitely the most majestic and inspiring of them all.

It has brought great joy to the children of Toa Payoh.

INSTANT EXPERT

Toa Payoh (twah pah-yoh)

In Hokkien, "toa" means "big", and "payoh" means "swamp". There's a similar word in Malay, "paya", which also means "swamp". A swamp is a muddy patch of ground, sometimes covered with water.

Tock-Tock Mee

There used to be travelling noodle sellers around Toa Payoh. They would hit two bamboo sticks together to make a sound. Parents gave their children money and sent them out to buy the "Tock-Tock Mee".

Chwee Kuay (ch-wee kway)

This is a small and delicious steamed cake made from rice flour. It is eaten with preserved vegetables and a bit of chilli paste. During the kampong days, many villagers made and sold chwee kuay for a living.

Toa Payoh Swimming Complex

Everyone was excited when it opened in 1973. There were three pools for the public to use, and two extra pools specially designed for water sports training. The best swimmers, divers and water polo players would come from all over Singapore to train here.

The Peter Low Choir

In the 1980s, the Church of the Risen Christ at Toa Payoh Central was known for having a great choir. The choir was led by Peter Low, a teacher. The Peter Low Choir gave many performances and also recorded its own music albums.

Toa Payoh Central Vertical Challenge

Block 79 at Toa Payoh Central is 40 storeys tall. The Toa Payoh Central Vertical Challenge is held here. Runners compete to see who can race to the top in the shortest time. There's even a special race where your pet can run along with you.

HAPPY DAYS IN TOA PAYOH

The Heartlands Exploration Group is happy to present this selection of photos from its collection.

In the 1950s, Muthu helped his father sell milk around the Toa Payoh kampongs. He was always pleased to meet a fellow LCAC member.

In 1972, a 25-metre tall tower was built in Toa Payoh Town Garden. If you climbed to the top, you could enjoy a great view all around. The Heartlands Exploration Group loved to have their meetings here.

According to neighbourhood legends, for over one hundred years the Chinese villagers would pay their respects to a very tall tree near Block 177. They believed that the tree brought them good luck and protected them. In 1965, the area was supposed to be cleared to make way for housing blocks. But when the bulldozers approached the tree, they would experience all sorts of problems. Other attempts to cut down the tree would be just as unsuccessful. The Heartlands Exploration Group assigned new member Dolly to write a report about this. The tree actually remained standing until 2013, when it was struck by lightning and came crashing down.

A Curious Feeling

It was a Saturday morning. Ling woke up feeling excited.

The Lion City Adventuring Club had its own private library at Toa Payoh Industrial Park. And it was her group's turn to clean up the place. Ling was looking forward to this. She loved to be around old books. She had some porridge for breakfast. And then her friend Shaya called.

"I am sorry," Shaya said, "my grandpa is ill. I have to stay home today and help look after him."

"That's okay," Ling said, "I hope he gets well soon!"

But after that there were two more calls. Brandon needed to attend a prize-giving event in school. And Reza had soccer training.

Ling was disappointed. There were only four people in her group. And the three others couldn't be there. Ling had nothing else planned for that day, so she decided to go down alone and do what she could.

"I'll drop you off after lunch," her father offered. "When you are done, give me a call and I'll pick you up."

Ling spent two hours opening up old boxes in the back room and making lists of everything she found inside.

Now she was down to the last box. She picked it up and and opened it. Inside, she found: six books about local food, four rolls of stickers with the LCAC logo, two thick files filled with LCAC membership details for the years 1973–78, a small tin of toffee sweets (still unopened), and a stack of old postcards.

And then something caught Ling's eye. She pulled it out and held it up. It was a faded photo of a brown notebook. Someone had drawn a question mark on it with a black marker. Which made it seem so mysterious. And somehow very important.

Ling felt a tingling on the back of her neck. It was as if she sensed the notebook calling to her. She had to find out more about it.

She turned the photo over, and saw a row of tiny stickers. Each sticker had one letter on it. The stickers were arranged to read:

OYStERS iN A hUG

Ling switched on the library computer and searched the folders until she found the information she wanted.

The Lion City Adventuring Club had over 20 storage spaces in Singapore and Malaysia. But the four main ones were in Queenstown, Marine Parade, Yishun and over in Penang.

Ling thought about the stickers behind the photo. She figured that they had originally been arranged in a different order. Someone probably thought it was funny to mess up the stickers like this.

Ling hurried over to the telephone and called Reza. "Hey," she said, "I discovered something cool today. Will you help me look for an old notebook? It's in one of our storage spaces. I know which one."

Do you know how Ling figured this out?
Clue: think about the stickers. Follow the story
in the next chapter to see if you're right.

SEE YOU AT THE TOWER!

Some members of the Lion City Adventuring Club are meeting at the Toa Payoh Town Park observation tower. They plan to explore the area and draw some maps of the place. Fan Fan wants to join them. But she's lost! Can you help her find her way?

CHAPTER 2

The History of
YISHUN

1947 Nee Soon Market was started. It was very popular, and grew very quickly. Because of this, the area got even more busy.

1956 Lim Nee Soon's son Lim Chong Pang was also a well-known businessman and a member of various government boards. When he passed away in 1956, the government changed the name of the nearby Westhill Village to Chong Pang Village to honour his memory.

1850 Landowners started new plantations around the mouth of the Seletar River. They hired lots of Chinese workers, who built more and more huts to live in. Eventually there were a lot of small villages all over the area.

1912 Lim Nee Soon opened factories and plantations here. He was so successful that the area began to be known as Nee Soon Village.

1976 This was the beginning of the Yishun New Town Project. Just like in Toa Payoh, the old villages here quickly gave way to high rise public housing, schools and factories. There was even a swimming pool and sports complex.

YISHUN
Where Lim Nee Soon was King

Way back in 1850, there were just a few plantations here. They grew mostly pepper and gambier. Pepper was used for cooking. Gambier was chewed, taken as medicine, or sometimes used to dye cloth.

The main village was called Chan Chu Kang. In those days, a Chinese village was called a "chu kang", and Chan was the name of the village headman.

In 1912, Lim Nee Soon opened the Thong Aik Rubber Factory here. He also bought over some of the land and started his own plantations. People soon gave him a grand nickname: Rubber and Pineapple King.

Many of the villagers here worked for Lim Nee Soon. They paid rent to live on his land. Soon everyone started calling this area Nee Soon Village. He was known to be a generous man.

There were many other villages here too, but those were not as well known.

LIM NEE SOON RUBBER FACTORY

Lim Nee Soon had a son who was very interested in movies. His name was Lim Chong Pang, and he ran two cinemas in this area. One was called Sultan Theatre, which opened in 1939. Around the same time, he took over an existing cinema and named it Seletar Cinema. Can you guess the cool nickname that the people gave him? Yup. He was called Cinema King.

In 1953, many Chinese villages had to leave their homes in Paya Lebar because the land was used to build a new airport. They moved to Chong Pang Village, near Nee Soon Village. The area got a lot more crowded.

Besides working for a living, the villagers also grew vegetables, kept pigs and chickens, and farmed everything from orchids to fish.

In 1976, the Singapore government came up with the Yishun New Town Project. They started to construct housing blocks, schools and factories here.

The Yishun Mass Rapid Transport (MRT) station opened in 1988. This made it a lot more convenient for the children living in Yishun to explore other parts of Singapore.

In 1992, the Yishun 10 cinema opened. It had ten screening rooms, each showing a different movie. Thanks to the MRT station across the road, people travelled here from all over the island to enjoy the movies.

Lim Nee Soon would have been so proud.

INSTANT EXPERT

Yishun

"Yishun" is the Chinese Hanyu Pinyin version of "Nee Soon".

Attap House

An attap house has walls made of wood, and a roof made from leaves of the attap palm tree. These houses were very popular in SIngapore and could be found all over Yishun until the 1960s.

Khatib MRT

There was once a village nearby known as Khatib Bongsu. It was along Sungei Khatib, or Khatib River. The MRT station was named after these places.

Statue Of Lim Nee Soon

If you go to Yishun Town Park, you'll see a statue of Lim Nee Soon. He lived from 1879 to 1936. He started his business empire when he was just 24 years old. He was also a community leader and donated a lot of money to the poor and sick.

Seletar Hot Springs

There is a hot spring just outside Yishun called the Seletar Hot Springs. The water is warm, and it smells odd. But many believe that the water has the ability to cure diseases. For over 100 years, people have travelled here to bathe in the water. The water was also bottled for drinking and sold under various brands.

MEMORIES OF YISHUN

The Heartlands Exploration Group found these interesting photos in its files.

In the 1960s, the area around Sultan Theatre was a popular gathering place for the LCAC members living in Chong Pang Village. Many people came here to watch movies, shop or eat at the coffee shops.

Fraser and Neave (F&N), the local soft drinks company, bottled the water from the Sembawang Hot Springs and sold it as Seletaris mineral water. Some LCAC members were forced to drink this, because their parents believed it would bring them good luck for their examinations. F&N stopped selling this around 1990.

LCAC members still enjoy exploring Yishun Park to catch a glimpse of the unusual birds, squirrels and monkeys that live there.

The Secret Notebook: Part 2
Strange Symbols

Ling saw Reza waiting for her outside the Yishun MRT station.

"What's this about?" Reza asked. "I hope it's not some silly game!"

She ran over and showed him the photo. She also told him about the stickers. Reza was intrigued.

"Oysters in a hug?" he said. "I ate some oysters when my parents took us to Thailand. But I didn't know they could give hugs."

"Look," Ling said to Reza, "if you rearrange the letters, this is what it says."

One by one, Ling peeled off the stickers and moved them around. When she was done, they spelt:

YISHUN STORAGE

Reza was impressed. "So that's why you asked me to meet you here!"

"You're the leader of the Heartlands Exploration Group, aren't you?" Ling said. "That means you have your own key to the Yishun storage space!"

❧

The storage space was in a building at the far end of Yishun. When they got there, Reza switched on all the lights. The space was about the size of three classrooms. It had eighteen rows of shelves, all stacked with boxes and bags of different sizes.

"We might be here all night," Reza said. He was starting to regret this. "The notebook could be in any one of these boxes!"

"Remember when I peeled off the stickers earlier?" Ling said. "There were some numbers written underneath in pencil. Twelve dash two."

Reza frowned. "That might mean it's the twelfth row, second shelf."

They hurried over. There were just four boxes on that shelf. They opened one box, then another, then one more. Ling pulled out some old magazines, and saw a brown envelope below them.

Her heart pounded harder.

"I think this is it," she said softly.

She picked up the envelope and opened it.

Sure, enough, there was a notebook inside. The same one she saw in the photo.

Ling's hands were trembling as she turned the pages. She was puzzled. The notebook was filled with writing, but she couldn't recognise any of the words. It seemed as if it was written in an alien language.

Reza took the notebook from Ling and studied the front and back covers.

"We need to find out who this belonged to," he said. "Maybe there's a name or membership number somewhere."

He held up the book and pointed to the top of the front cover.

"I think this is a clue," he said. "These symbols look like some kind of code."

Ling peered hard. Reza was right, there were two symbols there, drawn in blue ink. The first symbol looked like a campfire, with four pieces of wood sticking out from underneath. The second symbol looked like someone's leg, bent at the knee.

Ling shrugged. "What does this mean?"

"I'm not sure," Reza said. "But there's a familiar smell coming from the paper."

Ling sniffed hard. "You're right. It reminds me of my mother's dishwashing liquid."

Reza pinched his lip and thought hard. "It could be orange juice," he said. "Which means there's something here that we're not seeing."

What did Reza mean? Check the next chapter to find out.

SPOT THE DIFFERENCE

In the old days, the people of Nee Soon Village lived in attap houses that looked like this. Can you find five differences between the two pictures?

Answers: flowers in the bushes, boy with radio player; cat on roof; bird cage near door; window panel on the right.

CHAPTER 3

The History of QUEENSTOWN

Early 1900s This was a swampy area with a few villages. A popular name for this place was Bo Beh Kang. This is a Hokkien phrase that means "River Without a Tail". No matter how hard the villagers looked, they could never find where the river started. It was a big mystery.

1935 The Thye Hong Biscuit and Confectionery Factory opened. This was the first biscuit factory in Singapore. At that time it had the most impressive equipment anyone had ever seen, and it produced lots of yummy biscuits and sweets.

1952 The government developed this area as the first town outside the city. It was called Queenstown to honour Queen Elizabeth of Great Britain. She was Singapore's head of state then, as Singapore was a British colony.

1961 Some students at Queenstown Secondary Technical School started a band called The Quests. It would become one of Singapore's top rock and roll groups.

1970 Queenstown Branch Library was the first branch library to open in Singapore. The young bookworms living here were truly delighted.

QUEENSTOWN
Where Rock 'N' Roll Dreams Came True

Like most other parts of Singapore, this was once a swampy area. There was a prominent river that ran through it. There were hills on both sides of this river. There was a rubber plantation on one hill. On another hill, there was a cemetery.

Back then, most of the Chinese villagers living around here spoke Hokkien or Teochew. They lived in attap huts and grew their own food. As other parts of Singapore grew more crowded, more and more people moved here.

In 1935, the Thye Hong Biscuit and Confectionery Factory opened nearby. It produced all sorts of delicious biscuits that children loved.

The most popular one was probably the jam sandwich biscuit, which had two round biscuits held together by a thick and hard lump of jam. Most of the biscuits were shipped to other countries to be sold.

In 1954, the Alexandra Fire Station opened. It was kept busy for many years, putting out fires throughout the neighbourhood. In 1961 there was a great fire at Bukit Ho Swee, and firefighters from this station rushed over to help put it out.

By 1956, there were many new factories in Singapore, but not enough skilled workers to run them.

Queenstown Secondary Technical School was started to train young people so they they could get jobs in the factories.

In 1961, two of the students at this school learned to play the electric guitar, and started a rock 'n' roll band with their friends. Back then the school's newsletter was called "The Quest". This inspired the two musicians to call their group The Quests.

The Quests wrote their own songs. They also performed in other countries like Malaysia, Brunei and Hong Kong. They were treated like rock stars.

shanty gallopin'

In 1965, two cinemas opened here. One was the Golden City Theatre. The other was Venus Theatre. Queenstown residents came here to watch thrilling gongfu movies from Hong Kong. And sometimes the nearby schools would rent the auditoriums to hold their own events. Both cinemas closed in the 1980s.

In 1975, the Queensway Shopping Centre opened. Young athletes would come here after school and on weekends to buy all sorts of sports equipment. Soccer fans especially loved this place, because they could buy the jerseys of their favourite teams.

INSTANT EXPERT

Shuang Long Shan

In 1887, a group of Chinese immigrants bought a piece of land here to bury their dead relatives. They called this area Shuang Long Shan, which is Chinese for "Twin Dragons Hill".

Tanglin Halt Road

In the old days, this was part of the Tanglin district. And the Malayan Railway trains used to stop, or halt, here. That's how this road got its unusual name!

Shanty

This was the first hit song written and recorded by The Quests. When they released it in 1964, it quickly became the most popular song in Singapore. For a while, these boys were even more popular than The Beatles, a legendary band from England.

Queenstown Remand Prison

Did you know that there used to be a prison here? This was opened in 1966 because Outram Prison was getting too crowded.

Queenstown Swimming Complex

In the 1970s and 1980s, Queenstown had the most outstanding water polo team in Singapore. Kenneth Kee, their talented coach, recruited some beginners and trained them to represent Singapore in international swimming events. To many people, this seemed like a miracle.

QUEENSTOWN MEMORIES

This estate has been a truly amazing place.

In 1956, Forfar House was the tallest public housing flat in Singapore. It had 14 storeys. Residents and visitors were amazed to find that every kitchen had its own rubbish chute. Anything thrown inside would fall down the chute into a bin at the bottom. These would then be cleared by the estate cleaners. Previously the kampong dwellers had to get rid of their rubbish on their own. It was common to see rubbish sitting outside their homes for years and years.

The young people in Queenstown were very inspired when they found out about The Quests. They gathered their friends and started to make their own music. Some of the Lion City Adventuring Club members decided to form a band too. They performed at the Christmas party that year.

In the 1970s, the LCAC members organised their own swimming sessions at the Queenstown Swimming Complex. Previously they learnt to swim by diving into rivers and canals, which was very dangerous.

The First Name

The next day, after lunch, Ling and Reza went to Queenstown to look for Edward Low, their Senior Adventuring Mentor. He lived along a small street off Stirling Road.

Edward Low was surprised to see them. "What brings you all the way here?" he asked. "Is anything wrong?"

His son Justin went to get some drinks from the kitchen. And then Ling told them how Reza took the notebook into the male washroom, but the hand dryer wasn't working. So Reza asked Ling to go into the female washroom hold the notebook under the hand dryer.

"He insisted that there was something written in orange juice," Ling said. "But I was baffled. What did orange juice have to do with the hand dryer?"

Edward Low leant forward. There was a twinkle in his eyes. "Long ago, people used orange juice as an invisible ink," he explained, "for sending secret messages. When you use it to write on paper, there are no visible marks. But later, if you heat it up, the orange juice will turn brown, and the writing will appear."

"Yes!" Reza said. "We experimented with that in science class."

Edward Low turned to Ling. "So what was the message that appeared?

Ling held up the notebook. There was a string of numbers clearly visible now, followed by a word. "49—888 MERRILY"

"Could it be a telephone number?" Reza asked, trying to be helpful. "Or maybe the combination to a safe?"

Edward Low took a photo of the book cover with his mobile phone. "I'll look it up. Justin will call you if I find anything."

❧

A few days passed before Justin called Ling.

"It's a very old membership number," Justin said. "So old that my father couldn't recognise it. By the time he joined, membership numbers already had seven digits."

Justin explained that the old records were in the LCAC's bungalow in Penang. His father emailed them and they took a while to reply.

"Do you have a paper and pen ready?" Justin asked. "I can give you the member's name."

Ling could feel a surge of excitement rushing through her.

"It's a long shot," Ling said, "but I'm feeling lucky, so let me make a guess. Is the name — "

What do you think Ling said?
The story continues in the next chapter.

WORD SEARCH

On 12 September 2012, Prince William and his wife Catherine, the Duke and Duchess of Cambridge, visited Strathmore Green in Queenstown. Queenstown was named after Prince William's grandmother, Queen Elizabeth II. They also met with young artists at Rainbow Centre, which is a school for children with special needs.

Can you find these six words?

WILLIAM
CATHERINE
ROYALTY
QUEENSTOWN
VISIT
RAINBOW

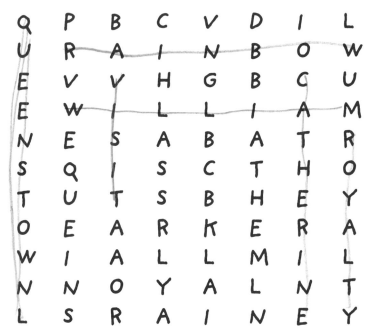

```
Q  P  B  C  V  D  I  L
U  R  A  I  N  B  O  W
E  V  V  H  G  B  C  U
E  W  I  L  L  I  A  M
N  E  S  A  B  A  T  R
S  Q  I  S  C  T  H  O
T  U  T  S  B  H  E  Y
O  E  A  R  K  E  R  A
W  I  A  L  L  M  I  L
N  N  O  Y  A  L  N  T
L  S  R  A  I  N  E  Y
```

Answers

CHAPTER 4
The History of
TIONG BAHRU

Early 1900s This area was known for its pig farms and Chinese cemetery.

1935 The government decided to clear the land and start building the first housing blocks in Singapore. Today, these blocks are still standing. They are considered to be very stylish, with their curved balconies and spiral staircases.

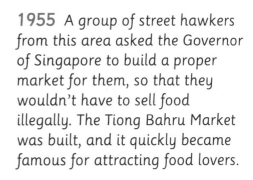

1951 Singapore's first community centre was built here. It encouraged people from the community to take part in healthy and useful activities, instead of gambling or fighting or wasting their time.

1955 A group of street hawkers from this area asked the Governor of Singapore to build a proper market for them, so that they wouldn't have to sell food illegally. The Tiong Bahru Market was built, and it quickly became famous for attracting food lovers.

1961 This was the year of the Bukit Ho Swee fire, one of the largest fires to happen in Singapore. It was a great tragedy that destroyed a school, shops, factories and wooden and attap houses. Four people died in the fire and about 16,000 people were made homeless.

TIONG BAHRU COMMUNITY CENTRE

TIONG BAHRU
How the Tomb Town came to Life

If you came here in the early 1900s, you would have found yourself wandering around a big mangrove swamp.

The most memorable landmark here was a Chinese cemetery. Back then, people came up with a name for this place by joining the Hokkien word for "cemetery" — "tiong" — with the Malay word for "new" — "bahru".

Yes, Tiong Bahru means "new tombs". This was a very important location to the Chinese because they believed they had to give their dead a good burial.

The successful businessman Tan Tock Seng was buried here. He died in 1850. You can still find his grave in Tiong Bahru. In fact, people make trips here just to have a look at it. It is of great historical interest.

In those days, besides the cemetery, there were a few squatter villages and farms around Tiong Bahru. Squatters are people who occupy a land or building without paying rent.

In 1925, the British government decided to clear the land and put it to better use. Almost 2,000 people were made to leave, and most of the graves dug out.

Lots of soil was brought here and added to the swampy ground to make it less mushy. In 1936, builders started work on the earliest block of modern flats. Some of these buildings were designed to look a little like ships. Other were long and looked like aeroplanes. They looked very charming and almost futuristic.

Families living here paid about $20 every month in rent. It was a big sum in those days. Soon the estate was a thriving place. It had its own market, shops and public spaces.

After World War Two, many more people moved here because of the good facilities. It got very crowded. By 1960, there were around 400,000 people here.

Tiong Bahru Park has been here since 1967. It now has its own Adventure Playground, which young explorers really love. You can wander through the maze, enjoy the swings, or crawl across the big wooden train that looks like something out of a funny movie.

Today, there are many new blocks of flats around Tiong Bahru. Unlike in the earlier days, the community here has become more diverse. There are also cafes, restaurants and interesting stores selling all sorts of cool stuff. Tourists love to shop here.

It's no longer a Tomb Town. It's full of life!

INSTANT EXPERT

Tan Tock Seng

He was born in Malacca and came to Singapore to sell vegetables. He learned to speak English, and started a business with a trader from England. In 1844, he donated money to build Tan Tock Seng Hospital. He is remembered for his success as a businessman, and his generosity in helping the sick.

Dancing Girl

This is a sculpture in Seng Poh Garden, which is in Tiong Bahru. The work was made by Lim Nang Sang in 1972. He was the sculptor who created the original Merlion statue. Some people stare and stare for a long time but they see only a jumble of shapes. They are not able to recognise the dancing girl. You need to look at the sculpture from just the right angle.

Bird Singing Corner

Tiong Bahru was once a bird lover's paradise with a corner for bird owners to gather. They would hang up their bamboo cages and let the birds compete, to see how beautifully each one could sing. It was so well-known that bird lovers from all over the world came to check it out. The huge frame for hanging bird cages is still standing, but today people have stopped bringing their birds here.

Wang Sa

A popular local comedian who could speak several dialects, Malay and English, Wang Sa used to live in Tiong Bahru. His real name was Heng Kim Ching and he often appeared on television with his performing partner, Ye Fong. They were known as "Ah Pui and Ah San", which meant "Fat One and Skinny One". Ye Fong was short and chubby, while Wang Sa was tall and thin.

TIONG BAHRU MEMORIES

More heartwarming photos from the Heartlands Exploration Group's albums.

It is an LCAC tradition to encourage new members to visit
Tan Tock Seng's grave in Tiong Bahru. They get to hike across
the neighbourhood and try out different foods along the way.
Many members remember this outing for years and years.

Mee pok is a popular Chinese
dish. It is made from flat noodles
and often served with fishballs or
minced meat, or sometimes both.
There is a mee pok stall at Moh
Guan Terrace, in Tiong Bahru, that
has been around for over 70 years.
LCAC members regularly organised
adventuring trips around this
neighbourhood just so that they
could have a meal here.

Sivalingam, the LCAC's sports secretary in the 1960s, was a huge fan of Wang Sa and Ye Fong. He learnt a few Chinese dialects from his neighbours so that he could understand the comedians' jokes better.

The Secret Notebook: Part 4

Face to Face

Ling and Reza walked around Tiong Bahru, looking for the address that Justin gave them.

"Mary Lee?" Reza said, for the seventh or eighth time. "Just like that, you guessed her name?"

Ling laughed. "It was a crazy hunch. My cousin does that too. Her name's Li Ping, and she signs off as 'Leaping'. So I just thought maybe 'Merrily' could be 'Mary Lee'."

Reza shook his head. "I can't believe she agreed to meet us. Do you think she'll be happy to see her old notebook again?"

"We'll find out soon," Ling replied. She pointed at a white building on the other side of the street. "Look, that must be her place. Justin said she's a bit eccentric, though. We'll need to give her time to remember things."

ᕥᔦᕤ

Mary Lee looked to be in her sixties. She invited them to have a seat while she prepared some snacks.

Ling took the old notebook out from her bag.

"Do you remember this?" Ling asked. "We found your membership number and name written in invisible ink. That's how we found you."

Ling thought Mary Lee would be thrilled to see the book again. But no. Mary put her cup of tea down quickly and her face turned pale. She almost choked.

"Where did you get that?" she asked, after a long silence.

Reza regretted surprising her like this. He explained everything.

Mary looked distressed. But after some time, she decided to tell them how the book was given to her.

"I joined the Lion City Adventuring Club in the early fifties," she said, blinking quickly as she tried to remember. "I helped to organise a few visits to the kampongs in the north. I remember that day very well. We were exploring part of the Seletar River. One of my older relatives lived in a small village at Nee Soon, and I hadn't seen him in a few months, so I thought I would pay him a visit."

Ling and Reza listened attentively. They had seen old photos of the area, and were imagining the scene in their heads.

"He didn't have much to say," Mary continued. She was close to tears. She picked up the notebook, very carefully, and turned the pages. It was almost as if she had forgotten that they were there with her. "He gave me this notebook and told me to learn from it. But if you look inside, you'll see that it's written in some strange language. I couldn't understand any of it. Was it a joke? He passed away a few weeks after that. I got really frustrated. I probably left it behind at one of the LCAC meetings, and someone packed it away."

"So your relative wrote all of this?" Ling asked. "Was he a teacher?"

"Why, no," Mary replied. "He worked as a gardener. He didn't go to school, and never learnt to read or write. But he was very good with his hands. He was always making things for the family, like tables and cupboards and toys."

Mary told them they could keep the notebook. She was too old now to do anything with it. And then she suddenly frowned. "Hold on. I think he did mention a name. Boh Eng Nee. But I've no idea who that might be."

"I have one last question, if you don't mind," Reza said politely. "What was your relationship with the person who gave you this notebook?"

"I had three relatives who lived near Nee Soon Village," Mary said, her mind drifting off again. "Uncle Soon lived in a red house. The one who lived in the white house was retired. Grand Uncle Yong owned a pig farm. And the one who repaired boats wasn't my Grandpa. I didn't visit the one in the green house or the one who repaired boats."

Can you work out which relative Mary Lee visited? You'll find the answer in the next chapter.

The Birds Of Tiong Bahru

The legendary singing birds of Tiong Bahru used to be a great neighbourhood attraction. They chirped merrily and tweeted with great zest. Can you solve this picture puzzle by figuring out the right order for these pieces, starting from the top left corner?

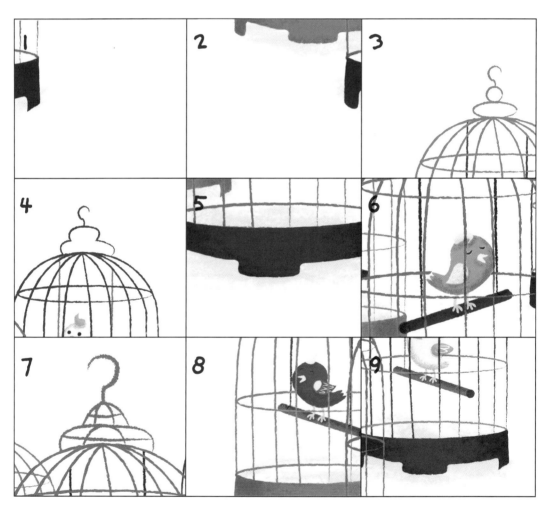

Answer

1	5	2
6	6	8
4	7	3

CHAPTER 5
The History of
KAMPONG BAHRU

1823 Temenggong Abdul Rahman moved to Kampong Bahru. He started a new village with his family and followers. He was an important man because he had helped Sir Stamford Raffles sign an agreement with Sultan Hussein Shah, which allowed the British to start a settlement in Singapore. "Temenggong" was his title. It was a position of great power.

1844 This area was labelled "Tulloh Blangan Hills" in a map drawn by John Turnbull Thomson. Mr Thomson was in charge of constructing roads and public buildings in Singapore.

1881 Rows of new shophouses as well as many bungalows were built. These were designed with a mix of European, Chinese and Malay architecture. Rich Chinese merchants and their families moved here.

1929 The Church of St Teresa was built. It is known for its beautiful architecture. Some people called this the "Hokkien Church", because many of the church-goers spoke Hokkien.

1932 The Keppel Road Railway Station opened. You could catch a train to Malaya here. The name was later changed to Tanjong Pagar Railway Station.

KAMPONG BAHRU
The Temenggong's New Home

Once upon a time, this area was called Tulloh Blangan Hills. There were seven hills here, and some of these reached as far as the area where Alexandra Road is today.

The hills had interesting names, like Bukit Purmei, which means "peaceful hill" in Malay; and Bukit Radin Mas, which means "hill of the princess of golden beauty", and was named after the Javanese princess, Radin Mas.

In 1823, Temenggong Abdul Rahman moved here to set up his own village. His family had a huge plot of land, and they were able to start a number of plantations. They grew spices and fruits. Soon, other kampongs also sprung up around here.

In 1845, the British decided to build a signal station on one of the hills. This was a tower with a set of flags, or moveable signs, which were used to send messages to ships in the area. It could be used to warn people of danger, or let them know about weather and tide conditions.

Captain Charles Edward Faber was put in charge of this project. He was given a team of convicts from India, and together they cleared the area and created a narrow road all the way up to the top of the hill.

After the work was done, the government named the hill Mount Faber, in memory of the Captain.

By 1881, there were more and more bungalows around the Spottiswoode Park area. Chinatown was too crowded, so the more prosperous families moved over to this area, which was quite serene in comparison.

In 1929, the Church of St Teresa was completed. It was considered to be Singapore's first rural church. Back then, the Bishop of Malacca was inspired to start this church for the community of Chinese Catholics from Fukien in China.

In 1932, the Keppel Road Railway Station was opened. This was built on reclaimed land. It was close to the docks at Tanjong Pagar , and goods could be transported quickly from the ships onto the trains, to be carried across to Malaysia. This train station stopped operating in 2011.

Today, there are housing blocks all along Kampong Bahru Road, from Spottiswoode Park Road to Silat Avenue and all the way down to Bukit Purmei. The old kampong of Temenggong Abdul Rahman has disappeared, but many of the beautiful houses from the old days are still standing. You should pay them a visit.

INSTANT EXPERT

Telok Blangah

This means "cooking pot bay" in Malay. A bay is a partly-enclosed area of water that is connected to the sea or ocean. When viewed from one of the hills, this bay looked like an Indian cooking pot.

Tanjong Pagar Railway Station

It took an international effort to build this. The construction company was from France, and the architect was from Serbia. An Italian sculptor created four giant statues for the facade. These represented Singapore's main money-making activities at that time: Agriculture, Commerce, Transport and Industry.

Keramat Radin Mas

This is a shrine dedicated to Princess Radin Mas Ayu, who sacrificed her own life in order to protect her father. The shrine is near Mount Faber. In 1959, there was a Malay film made about her, titled, Raden Mas.

De La Salle School

This boys' school opened in 1952 and was a popular choice for the children living in this area. The school has since moved to Choa Chu Kang.

National Monuments

The Church of St Teresa is a national monument. The building design was inspired by a church in France, the Basilica of the Sacred Heart of Paris. The Tanjong Pagar Railway Station is also a national monument. National monuments are buildings or places that are protected by the government because they played an important part in our history.

KAMPONG BAHRU SNAPSHOTS

Kampong days were happy days.

Baba House, just a short distance off Kampong Bahru Road, was once the home of a Peranakan family. The Peranakan people are also known as Straits Chinese. They were originally immigrants from China who settled down here and adopted some local ways of living. The men are called Baba, and the women are called Nyonya. Visiting Baba House is like stepping back in time, because you get to experience how the Peranakan families lived in the old days.

There were many kampongs along the railway tracks. The villagers here often made their living working at the railway station, or selling food to the passengers. These kampongs were great places to explore and make new friends.

Mount Faber Park is a very old park, one of the oldest on this island. You can catch a cable car from here and travel across to Sentosa. It's a great adventure, but definitely not for those afraid of heights.

The Secret Notebook: Part 5
The Friend

Ling and Reza returned to their Toa Payoh library to continue their research.

Reza just couldn't figure out what Mary Lee meant. So Ling explained it to him.

"She said she had three relatives living there," Ling said. "This is what we know: one of them lived in a white house, and was retired. Her Grand Uncle Yong had a pig farm. And her Uncle Soon lived in the red house."

Reza nodded. "Yes. Do continue."

"If you analyse the rest of the information," Ling said, "it's clear that Grand Uncle Yong must have lived in the green house. And Uncle Soon was the one who repaired boats. She said she didn't visit those two. So she must have visited the one in the white house. And that must have been her Grandpa!"

Reza slapped his forehead. He looked relieved. "Thanks! I finally get it!"

Ling sat back. She twirled her hair with her fingers, lost in thought. "Now we need to figure out, who on earth was Boh Eng Nee?"

They spent the rest of the afternoon searching the internet for this name. They found nothing. But according to an old newspaper article, in the seventies a person named Boh Teng Gee was interviewed by a reporter at Blair Road.

❧

The next morning they met at the Outram Park MRT station. They walked over to Kampong Bahru Road, and turned into Blair Road. The place was very quiet. There didn't seem to be any old residents that they could talk to.

"This is a waste of time!" Ling finally admitted. "What should we do now?"

Reza nodded. "I meant to tell you, I had a thought last night. I've a former classmate named Fernandes Ho. He's an LCAC member too. He's very good with puzzles and mysteries. I think he can help us make sense of the strange writing in the notebook."

Ling sighed. "I truly believe that we're meant to solve this. But it's more difficult than I expected."

Reza hesitated for a bit. "You know, I was thinking about the two symbols on the cover. The campfire and the leg. It could be a name."

Ling looked at him in disbelief. She pulled out the notebook and stared at the symbols. "Why do you say that?"

What was Reza's response?
You'll find out in the next chapter.

THE GREAT SCRAMBLE

Can you unscramble these five phrases and figure out the original words or names? They're all mentioned in this chapter.

1. RUB MIKE I PUT
(CLUE: A HILL)

2. A RAG BUMP HONK
(CLUE: A VILLAGE)

3. GO THANK A BELL
(CLUE: A BAY)

4. GENT ME GONG
(CLUE: A PERSON'S TITLE)

5. EAR TESTS
(CLUE: A CHURCH)

Answers:
1. Bukit Purmei
2. Kampong Bahru
3. Telok Blangah
4. Temenggong
5. St Teresa

CHAPTER 6

The History of JALAN KAYU

Mid-1800s Chinese farmers and plantation owners settled down here. They grew gambier, pepper and vegetables.

1928 The British built a Royal Air Force base at Seletar. It was the first of its kind to be located outside the United Kingdom.

1970s There were pig farms and a few blocks of flats here. In 1975, a new market and hawker centre was built along Seletar Road. But on the whole, it was a quiet neighbourhood. Many families live here for a long time, and the community felt like one big village.

1942 During World War Two, when the Japanese occupied Singapore, they named this airbase Seretar Hikojo ("Seletar Airport").

2000s This area looked more modern, especially with the new Fernvale public housing estate, which is part of Sengkang New Town. Part of the airbase was converted into a new Seletar Aerospace Park. This is where aeroplane engines are repaired.

JALAN KAYU
Planes and Prata

Did you know that "Jalan Kayu" is Malay for "wooden road"? In the old days this road used to get extremely muddy, and the villagers had to lay their own logs and planks along the way so that they could walk across the muddy patches without getting dirty.

By 1900, there were many villages and farms around here. Some of these would survive even until the 1980s. One well-known village was called Yio Chu Kang. There is still a road now named after it.

In the early 1920s, the British thought they needed an airbase in the north of Singapore. They also planned to build a naval base near here, for their ships.

They ended up choosing Seletar as the site for the new airbase. "Seletar" was actually the name of a sea village tribe that used to live along the Straits of Johor. This area was named after them.

In 1928, Seletar Airbase was completed. It was the biggest Royal Air Force base in this part of the

world. The first aircraft to land here were four seaplanes, also affectionately called "flying boats".

At first, this airbase was the only airport in Singapore. It was soon serving both military as well as civilian passengers. Jalan Kayu was the main road leading to it. For this reason, it was a very important road.

After the Japanese left Singapore at the end of World War Two, the British took control of the airbase again, until they too left this island in 1971. Part of this airbase was then taken over by the Singapore Armed Forces, while the rest was used by private aviation companies.

During this time, many of the people who lived here either worked on the airbase, or ran the shops and restaurants around it.

In 1975, the Seletar Market and Food Centre was opened. It quickly became a busy place because residents from Ang Mo Kio, Hougang, Serangoon and Thomson would come all the way here to get their fresh food.

One morning in 2000, there was a big fire that burned down part of the market. It took some time to complete the repairs, and soon the market was bustling again. It was finally closed for good in 2004. Some of the stall owners had been serving customers in this area for many decades. They were sad but they had to move on.

After this, the neighbourhood transformed quite rapidly into a modern heartland. In the 2000s, the Fernvale housing estate was built next to Jalan Kayu. It's part of Sengkang New Town. And the airbase has now become Seletar Aerospace Park.

Even with these changes happening all around, you can still walk down Jalan Kayu now and imagine the old days when children had to step carefully from one plank to another on their way to school.

And if you should get hungry, you can visit one of the legendary Jalan Kayu prata shops and try the delicious crispy prata that many people associate with this neighbourhood.

INSTANT EXPERT

Mr C. E. Wood

From 1927, he supervised the construction of the Seletar Airbase. People were impressed when he turned the swampy area into a landing strip. His name, Wood, is translated into Malay as "kayu". Some people claim that Jalan Kayu was named after him.

Seletar Airport

Long ago, this was the only place in Singapore for planes to take off and land. It also served as the island's airport for civilian passengers, until Kallang Airport opened in 1937. The famous comedian Charlie Chaplin was one of the celebrity passengers who landed at Seletar. He is known for his many silent films.

Amelia Earhart

Born in 1897, she was an American pilot and adventurer. She was the first woman to fly alone over the Atlantic Ocean. She tried to fly around the world. As part of this journey, she landed at Seletar Airbase in June 1937. Sadly, the next month her plane disappeared somewhere over the Pacific Ocean.

Sengkang New Town

The estate was named after a road here, Lorong Senkang. "Sengkang" is Chinese for "auspicious harbour". There used to be a big fishing village here, as well as pineapple and rubber plantations.

Roti Prata (Ro-Tee Prah-Tah)

This is an Indian pancake that is served with thick curry, or sometimes sugar. Today, it is also made with eggs, banana, cheese, mushroom or chocolate sauce inside. Jalan Kayu has many shops that sell prata.

DREAMS OF FLYING

Jalan Kayu was an exciting place to explore, especially if planes fascinated you.

Back then, even up to the 1980s, children were thrilled to see or hear a plane flying near them. If they were in school and they heard one nearby, they might run out of the class to take a look, even in the middle of a lesson. Many LCAC members were plane enthusiasts. They loved to hang out around Seletar Airbase so they could get a glimpse of these shiny flying machines.

In the old days, Seletar Airport didn't have a fence around it. Animals from the neighbouring farms might sometimes wander across the runway as a plane was preparing to take off.

After a busy day of adventuring in the north of Singapore, LCAC members would often meet at Jalan Kayu for a prata party. The prata here was known to be especially crispy and tasty. Some of the shops would even be open through the night. Imagine how much prata you could eat!

The First Page

They met Fernandes Ho at a prata shop along Jalan Kayu.

Fernandes was a big boy with very short hair and muscular shoulders, from swimming a lot. He ordered two egg pratas and a big dish of curry chicken.

"Keep talking," he mumbled as he ate. "Don't worry, I'm listening."

"Reza figured out what the symbols mean," Ling said. "It's a kind of code. The campfire means 'burn'. And the leg is bent at the 'knee'. Once you put both together, it says 'Bernie'. I think."

Fernandes nodded. Now he looked more interested. "It's a rebus puzzle. Using pictures to represent sounds."

"See?" Reza said to Ling. "I told you he knows a lot."

Ling showed Fernandes the first page of the notebook.

"Can you help us figure out what this means?"

Fernandes actually put down his fork and spoon to examine the words.

This was what he saw:

Aol Thubhs vm Olhclusf Pucluapvuz
Av jylhal h Olhclusf Pucluapvu, fvb tbza
ohcl h jslhy pthnpuhapvu huk h iyhcl
olhya. Fvby dvyr dpss aolu il bzlmbs,
ilhbapmbs, wvdlymbs huk jslcly.

Fernandes spent a few minutes counting quietly with his fingers. Ling and Reza waited eagerly. Would Fernandes be able to make sense of this?

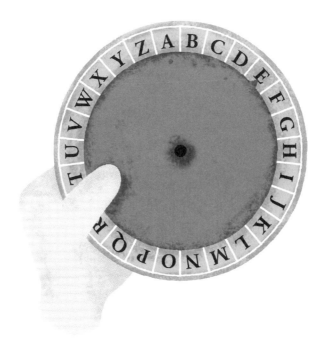

Finally, Fernandes smiled.

"Easy," he said. "This is called a Caesar code. The Roman general Julius Caesar used it a lot. You take your original message, and shift each letter down the alphabet a certain number of steps. To decode the message, just move the letters backwards again."

Ling and Reza looked at each other and exchanged shrugs. They didn't really understand him.

Fernandes finished his food and stood up. "I need to go to the gym. If you move the three letters of the first word back seven letters, you get 'the'. Now try work out the rest of the text on your own. See you!"

He went over to the cashier and paid for his meal. Then he hoped on his bicycle and pedalled away.

Can you decode the text shown on the opposite page? Head over to the next chapter and see if you're right.

WHAT'S THE MESSAGE?

Did you know that back then, an airbase would use Morse code to communicate with pilots in the air? This worked by changing each letter into a sequence of dots and dashes. The dots and dashes would then be transmitted over a radio set using simple blips. A dot would be one blip, while a dash would be three blips. We've prepared an urgent message for you in Morse code. How quickly can you decode this?

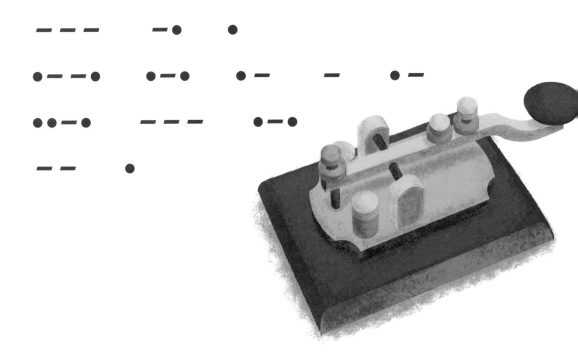

Key for International Morse Code

A	● —	H	● ● ● ●	O	— — —	V ● ● ● —
B	— ● ● ●	I	● ●	P	● — — ●	W ● — —
C	— ● — ●	J	● — — —	Q	— — ● —	X — ● ● —
D	— ● ●	K	— ● —	R	● — ●	Y — ● — —
E	●	L	● — ● ●	S	● ● ●	Z — — ● ●
F	● ● — ●	M	— —	T	—	
G	— — ●	N	— ●	U	● ● —	

CHAPTER 7
The History of
MARINE PARADE

1951 The original seawall along the beach was damaged. A seawall is a man-made wall that prevents the crashing waves from damaging the shore. The seawall was repaired to save the roads and buildings nearby. The city council built walkways, benches and changing rooms for the public to use. Marine Parade became a beautiful beach hangout.

1920 Moona Kadir Sultan, a merchant from India, started a business selling cattle in Singapore. He built a beautiful house here. This building later became The Grand Hotel. Many homes in this area were owned by rich Eurasian and Peranakan families.

1945 After World War Two, the beach was a mess. There was rubbish and wreckage everywhere, and the water was oily. Still, people came here to enjoy the open space and the view.

1966 The government shipped earth from Bedok and Siglap to fill the sea here. The coastline was extended further and further out. The Marine Parade housing estate was built on this land. So was the East Coast Park.

1980s East Coast Park becomes a hip weekend destination. People from all over Singapore come here to cycle, skateboard, enjoy barbecues, fly kites, windsurf as well as swim.

MARINE PARADE
People of the New Land

Two hundred years ago, Marine Parade didn't exist. Not the park, not the housing estate. Not even the land.

Back then, the sea started a lot further in. The beach was actually close to where the Katong area is today.

The earliest buildings here were plantation houses and bungalows. There were also a few kelongs nearby. A kelong is a hut for fishing that is built over the sea.

One of the more impressive landmarks was a big mansion built by Moona Kadir Sultan in 1920. He named it Karikal Mahal, which means "Palace of Karikal". He was originally from the town of Karikal in India. People often described his home as majestic.

Another legendary landmark was a bright red building along East Coast Road. It was often called the Red House. In 1925, a Jewish man started a bakery here. Some years later, he sold this to a sailor from the Hainan region in the south of China. The business was called Katong Bakery & Confectionery, but people referred to it as the Red House Bakery. It sold great cakes, buns and pastries.

After World War Two, the British soldiers spent a lot of time cleaning up the beach, because it was common to find bombshells left behind by the Japanese army. These could have exploded at any time.

They did such a good job that the beach became a terrific spot for all sorts of gatherings and adventures. People came here to enjoy the sun, sea and sand, and also the relaxing sea breeze.

In the 1950s, there was a big effort to make it even more beautiful and family-friendly. It started to look like a beach resort town. There were cinemas, shops and interesting places to eat. Sadly, many of these are no longer around.

From the 1960s onwards, there was a long project to reclaim the land and create more space to build homes for the people. This was called "The Great East Coast Reclamation". It lasted for 22 years.

The Marine Parade housing estate was then created on this amazing new land. It has its own town centre, cosy homes, schools, shops, offices and a lovely beach park for all sorts of outdoor activities.

To many people, this seemed like a great miracle.

INSTANT EXPERT

Francis James Bernard

In 1823, Mr Bernard set up a coconut plantation here. He was Chief of the Police Force, and looked after the storerooms near the harbour. He also started country's first newspaper, the Singapore Chronicle. His father-in-law was William Farquhar, the first person appointed by Stamford Raffles to manage Singapore.

Katong Laksa

Laksa is a noodle dish commonly found in this region. According to local folklore, back in the 1950s there was a hawker here who created his own laksa dish to sell to the hungry beachgoers. He cut the laksa noodles into shorter strips so that customers could eat them with just a Chinese spoon. Other hawkers copied his laksa recipe and also snipped their noodles before serving.

East Coast Parkway

This expressway runs between the city and Changi Airport. It connects the people of Marine Parade with the city. It is especially beautiful because of the sea view and rows of beautiful trees along the way.

Joo Chiat Road

This former private road called Confederate Estate Road was owned by Chew Joo Chiat. He was a businessman who grew pepper, nutmeg, gambier and coconut on his plantations here. In 1917, he donated this land to the government for them to build a road for cars. They named the road after him.

FOOD AND FUN

We love exploring the Marine Parade neighbourhood!

The LCAC loved to meet for breakfast at the Katong Bakery & Confectionery. They sold fresh kaya toast, swiss roll, curry puff, and more.

East Coast Park has always been a fascinating place to spend our weekends and make new friends. We would sometimes come across strange items in the sand, like unusual coins or odd-looking bottles or pretty seashells.

Katong laksa is so popular that it is now sold all over Singapore, not just in Katong. But if you really want to enjoy the full experience, you must eat it at one of the charming roadside stalls here.

Another Clue

Reza lived in Marine Parade. They went to his place to work out the rest of the text. The first few sentences read:

The Manual of Heavenly Inventions

To create a Heavenly Invention, you must have a clear imagination and a brave heart. Your work will then be useful, beautiful, powerful and clever.

Ling hugged herself. "This is exciting!" she squealed. "We're so close to finding the person who owned this notebook. I can feel it!"

Just then, Reza's mobile phone rang. He went to get it from his bag. He didn't recognise the caller's number, but he thought he should take the call anyway.

When he was done, his face beaming.

"Who was that?" Ling wanted to know. "Why are you grinning like it's your birthday?"

"That was Mary Lee," Reza said. "She somehow remembered that her Grandpa had given her not one notebook, but two. So she went to search inside her storeroom. And she found it!"

Ling felt her heart leap with joy. She couldn't wait to get hold of the other notebook. What did it contain?

"Mary says we can pick it up from her place," Reza continued. "In the meantime, she'll send us some photos."

A few minutes later, Reza's phone beeped. There was a new message. He opened it and saw the first photo from Mary. It showed four strips of paper. Reza realised that it was probably a page from the notebook, that had been torn up.

"Huh?" Ling exclaimed when she saw it. "What's this supposed to say?"

How should the strips be arranged?
The answer's in the next chapter.

KNOW YOUR KATONG LAKSA

Laksa is a delicious noodle dish. There are many ways to prepare laksa. The Katong style of laksa comes with a thick curry. It is truly yummy. Can you identify all the ingredients in this bowl? Draw a line to connect each word to the right item in the picture.

INGREDIENTS:

* thick rice noodles
* coconut milk curry made with spices
* prawns
* fish cake
* laksa leaves (sometimes called Vietnamese mint)
* sambal (chilli with shrimp paste)
* tau pok (fried beancurd puffs)

CHAPTER 8
The History of PUNGGOL

Before 1800s. There was a fishing village known as Kampong Punggol here. This village was thriving long before Stamford Raffles came to Singapore.

1828 Raffles got Captain James Franklin and Lieutenant Philip Jackson to create a map of the island, dividing it into different districts. On this map, they labelled Punggol as "Tanjong Rangon".

Mid-1800s Chinese settlers grew rubber and started farms. There was a market here where they sold their chicken, fish, vegetables and fruit. This was a popular place for the farmers and fishermen to meet.

1930s The seafood restaurants around Punggol Jetty became famous for serving delicious chilli crabs. People also came here to rent boats so they could explore the area and enjoy activities such as diving and fishing.

1990s onwards The farms and other businesses were closed down to make way for two public housing estates: Sengkang New Town and Punggol New Town. The Punggol Waterway Park was also created. This park has space for many family activities. There are also trees that have survived from the old days of Punggol.

PUNGGOL
The Fish and Fruit Paradise

From the early days, there was a lot of activity along Sungei Serangoon, or Serangoon River. This was the river that ran through Punggol. You could get a ride on a sampan, which is a small and flat boat, and travel up and down this river.

The original settlement here was a Malay fishing village. And then, around 1850, lots of Chinese immigrants moved here to become farmers. They kept mostly chicken and pigs. They also started rubber plantations here.

In the old days, if you were walking along a path and came across a fruit tree, you might grab the nearest stick and throw it at the branches, and hope that some juicy mangoes or rambutans might fall off and land at your feet.

Believe it or not, that's how Punggol got its name. In Malay, it means "throwing sticks". Punggol used to be filled with forests and farms with lots of edible fruit. People would chuck sticks at the trees, hoping to knock off something ripe and juicy.

There was a big Catholic community here too. In 1853, an attap hut was converted into the Church of the Nativity of the Blessed Virgin Mary, and it attracted many of the Teochew farmers around here.

There was a sad incident at Punggol Beach during the World War Two. After the British surrendered, the Japanese soldiers were afraid that the Chinese would rise up against them. So they gathered many young Chinese men at Punggol Beach, and shot them. This was known as the Punggol Beach Massacre.

After the war ended, the government developed this area further. The people soon enjoyed proper roads, electricity, water pipes and drains.

In 1963, Television Singapore started broadcasting. The villagers in Punggol were able to install antennas to watch different TV programmes. They felt more connected with the rest of the island.

This lasted until the 1980s, when many of the farmers had to move out and make way for two new housing estates, Sengkang New Town and Punggol New Town.

Sungei Serangoon is now Serangoon Reservoir. The fishing village is gone, and the fruit farms have disappeared too. Today, Punggol is a modern waterfront town with lots of new water sports facilities and stylish homes. Even then, we still remember the good old days of the past.

INSTANT EXPERT

Punggol Point

This is a popular spot for taking photos, fishing and watching the sun rise. Punggol Jetty is located here too. A jetty is a special platform for boats to pick up passengers.

Punggol Beach Massacre

The Japanese army killed about 400 Chinese men here. There were also other massacre sites around Singapore, including Changi Beach, Hougang and Siglap.

Coney Island

This small island near Punggol is also known as Pulau Serangoon. "Coney" is another word for "rabbit". Other places around the world are also called Coney Island.

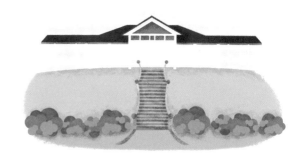

Matilda House

This big bungalow at Punggol Road was built by the Cashin family in 1902. They were originally from Ireland, and owned a lot of land in Singapore. The family no longer lives here. The bungalow was left empty and there were even rumours that it was haunted. There are plans to restore the bungalow and allow visitors to tour the place.

Natural Treasures

As nature lovers, the LCAC is very interested in wildlife. Because of the recent building projects here, the original swamps have been cleared away. This has disturbed the natural life cycles of the plants and animals. We hope that these natural treasures can be protected for future generations to appreciate.

FOOD AND FUN

Over the years, the LCAC has organised many exciting outings to the Punggol neighbourhood.

In the old days, some of us made our own maps so that we could go back to our favourite durian trees. If you were patient enough, and lucky, you might find a spiky treat waiting for you.

The restaurants here were known for their spicy chilli crabs. The yummy sauce was made from tomato ketchup and chilli, mixed with other ingredients to add more flavour. This sauce is best enjoyed with fluffy white rice or bread.

Matilda House always seemed like a such a cool and mysterious place, especially after it had been empty for a long time. LCAC members looked forward to visiting it and writing about their experiences in their journal.

House of Mystery

The next day, Ling and Reza collected the notebook from Mary Lee.

This notebook was filled with sketches of a house, from every possible angle. And on the last page someone had scribbled with a thick red marker: "Destroyed in Fire".

Thanks to the first photo that Mary sent them, they knew the sketches were of Matilda House, the well-known bungalow in Punggol.

When Ling and Reza got there, they found the area completely fenced up. There was construction work going on.

"There's nothing for us to see here," Ling said. She was disappointed. "I did some research this morning. Matilda House wasn't destroyed in any fire. I'm sure of that."

Reza took out his mobile phone. He had stored a memo on it, listing all their steps in this investigation so far. He scrolled down slowly, point by point, thinking hard.

"There's something else we can look into," he said. "Remember the two symbols on the first notebook? The one that said 'Bernie'? What if we added that in front of the name that Mary gave us?"

"Like, 'Bernie' plus 'Boh Eng Nee'?" Ling asked.

"Let's see if we can find anyone named Bernie Boh!" Reza said. He kicked himself for not thinking of this before.

⁂

After much digging online, the only Bernie Boh they could find was a retired Singapore businessman.

He had taken over his father's business at a young age and grew this into the BB Cardboard Corporation. At one point, he was known as the Cardboard King of Southeast Asia.

After retirement, he spent his time working with a group of volunteers to teach children how to design simple cardboard robots.

"I bet these two notebooks belonged to him!" Ling said. "I don't know why, or how, but I can just feel it."

"Let's contact his volunteer group," Reza suggested, "maybe they can help us."

The group was called Boards & Bots. There was an email address on their website. Reza and Ling sent them a message. They mentioned the two notebooks, and asked if Bernie Boh might know anything about them.

Half a day later, the reply came.

"Bernie wants to meet you at our workshop," the email said. "Would you be free this Saturday?"

Ling and Reza gave themselves a few minutes to let it all sink in.

"I can't wait to see his face when we hand him the notebooks," Reza said. "That would be a moment to remember!"

Ling examined the second notebook again. She was moved by the drawings inside. It was clear how much the artist loved the Matilda House. The passion showed in every sketch.

"As a boy, Bernie was probably enchanted by this house," Ling said slowly. "And then the notebook said it was destroyed in a fire. But at the same time, it's still standing today. How can this be?"

Indeed, how can this be? Find out in the next section.

THE KING OF FRUITS

Did you know that people across Southeast Asia call the durian, the "King of Fruits"? It's very popular in Singapore. You can still find durian trees in some parts of Punggol. Colour this durian stall and make it as pretty as you can.

The Cardboard King

The Boards & Bots workshop occupied two floors in a building along Bukit Timah Road.

Ling and Reza got there about ten minutes early. But Bernie Boh was already waiting for them at the reception area.

He was a jolly looking man with a chirpy voice. He introduced himself and told them how much he had been looking forward to this.

"If you don't mind," he said softly, "may I see the old notebooks that you found?"

Reza took them out from his bag, and handed them over.

Bernie silently examined them. He stared at every page, as if he couldn't believe what he was seeing.

And when he finally looked up again, his eyes were filled with tears of joy.

"Thank you," he said. "Now let me tell you my story."

cardboard to Matilda House. He loved the place. He decided to create his own cardboard model of it, and enter it in an art and craft competition.

Bernie spent many weeks sketching in his notebooks, and making plans for his model. One day, his family's gardener noticed him. This happened to be Mary's grandfather, Grandpa Lee.

Grandpa Lee came to Singapore when he was a young man. He worked as a coolie at first, and later a gardener. In his younger days, though, back in China, he used to be an apprentice to a paper craftsman, making fans and lamps and toys. He couldn't read or write, but he was able to memorise lots of books that his master read to him.

Grandpa Lee had a longing to share some of his papercraft skills. So he decided to help Bernie. He told Bernie about the Manual of Heavenly Inventions. This was an ancient book that contained advice on how to be creative and make all sorts of wonderful things.

Bernie wrote down everything that Grandpa Lee taught him, but in code, to keep it a secret from his four older brothers. This was the text of first chapter:

When Bernie was young, he wanted to be an architect. His dream was to design buildings and build amazing playgrounds for children.

But his father was against this. His father owned a shop that supplied all sorts of cardboard. He wanted Bernie to work for him and run a cardboard factory one day.

One day, when Bernie was still a teenager, he had to deliver some

The Manual of Heavenly Inventions

To create a Heavenly Invention, you must have a
clear imagination and a brave heart. Your work
will then be useful, beautiful, powerful and clever.
Whether creating a book or building a great city,
the method is the same.

★ First, it must be imagined.
★ Second, it must be assembled carefully.
★ Third, it must be shared with the world,
and protected from those who are
jealous, clumsy or ignorant.

So that the people might enjoy what you make.
Those who follow this path can be truly wealthy.

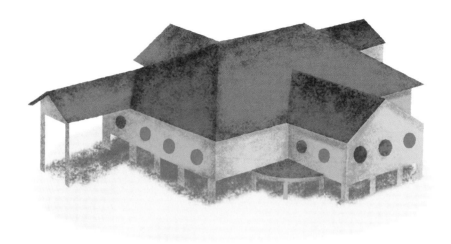

One day, Bernie's father discovered that the gardener had been spending time with Bernie. He got angry and threw Bernie's notebooks away. He also sacked the gardener.

Bernie finished the cardboard model of Matilda House on his own. There was a wooden shed behind his home, and he worked there. But there was a fire one day, and the shed burnt down. It was too late for Bernie to make another model for the competition.

Bernie did take over his father's business, and became very successful.

Later on, he regretted not searching for Grandpa Lee when he was younger. But it was too late.

⁂

When Ling got home that evening, she told her father everything.

"Grandpa Lee somehow managed to save the notebooks," she explained. "He gave them to his granddaughter Mary Lee, hoping that she might be able to learn something from them. Since he was illiterate, he couldn't tell that the text was written in code. Mary couldn't figure out what the writing meant. She got frustrated, and forgot all about it."

Ling's father was very quiet. He gave Ling a gentle pat on her head. "You did well," he said. "I'm glad you didn't give up your search, and managed to return the notebooks to Bernie Boh."

Ling was surprised by what her father said next.

"When I was young, we were poor," he said. "Every weekend I would work at a coffeeshop in Toa Payoh. I wiped tables and washed dishes. The owner's name was Madam Chua. She was a stern woman. But she was kind to me, and taught me many things about life. I often wondered what happened to her. Maybe I should look for her. I would like to thank her, and see if she needs any help in her old age. Will you and your friends help me?"

Ling quickly gave her father a hug.

She couldn't wait to get started.

A few weeks after this, Bernie Boh met with Edward Low to see how he could support the LCAC's heartlands research work. At the end of the session, he wrote a cheque and handed this to Edward.

"Please accept this as a small gesture of my gratitude," Bernie said.

"There are many more secrets waiting for us in the heartlands. Our work has only just begun."

ABOUT THE AUTHOR

Don Bosco writes stories for children and teens. Although grown-ups do read and enjoy them too. These are mostly influenced by the mystery, thriller, science fiction, adventure, fantasy and joke books he enjoyed as a child.

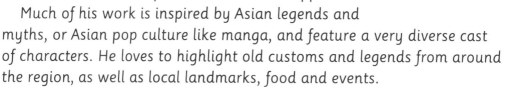

He started the publishing studio Super Cool Books in 2011, after his two sons challenged him to create a fantasy series for children, set in Singapore and Malaysia. That eventually grew into the Time Talisman series, which led to more and more books. The titles are available on the Super Cool Books iPad app.

Much of his work is inspired by Asian legends and myths, or Asian pop culture like manga, and feature a very diverse cast of characters. He loves to highlight old customs and legends from around the region, as well as local landmarks, food and events.

Don lives in Singapore but seems to spend most of his time either wandering around inside his head or searching the internet to discover new music to listen to. His website is http://www.SuperCoolBooks.com.

ABOUT THE ILLUSTRATOR

Sharon Lei is a fun-sized girl. Born and raised in Macau, she studied design in Singapore. She believes that getting immersed in different cultures will widen her horizons and inspire greater creativity. For that reason, she

loves traveling and hopes to see more of the world. Sharon is a hungry monster – constantly hunting for food and challenges. She enjoys the adrenaline rush that comes from receiving exciting briefs and award-winning projects, even if it means staying up all night to explore ideas.

When she's not busy crafting creative solutions, Sharon is likely to be found stalking stray cats. She posts doodles on instagram about cats and dogs tackling first world problems (@Maoandpuff).

ALSO AVAILABLE

EXPLORE SINGAPORE, LEARN COOL STUFF & SOLVE MINI-MYSTERIES

LION CITY Adventures

DON BOSCO

ENTER THE EXCITING WORLD OF THE LION CITY ADVENTURING CLUB!

Come join us and explore these 10 very special locations around Singapore. You will learn all sorts of cool stuff about each place.

But that's not all. With the Lion City Adventuring Club, there are always mysteries to solve and challenges to crack.

Will you complete your adventures and earn your certificate?

YOUR 10 LION CITY ADVENTURES

- Singapore River
- Geylang Serai
- Chinatown
- Little India
- Kampong Glam
- Singapore Flyer
- Gardens by the Bay
- Singapore Discovery Centre
- Singapore Botanic Gardens
- Mint Museum of Toys